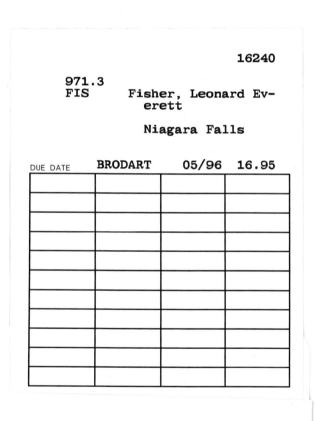

16240

971.3
FIS   Fisher, Leonard Ev-
               erett

          Niagara Falls

DUE DATE   **BRODART**   05/96   16.95

FALLS OF NIAGARA.

Above, below, where'er the astonished eye
Turns to behold, new opening wonders lie,

There the broad river, like a lake outspread,
The islands, rapids, falls, in grandeur dread.

With uproar hideous first the *Falls* appear:
The stunning tumult thundering on the ear.

This great, o'erwhelming work of awful Time,
In all its dread magnificence, sublime.

Falls of Niagara: Edwin Hicks, circa 1830
Hicks visited the falls in 1819. He made this oil painting
for his doctor. The couplets that border the art are from
Alexander Wilson's poem, "The Foresters."

Abby Aldrich Rockefeller Folk Art Center,
Williamsburg, Virginia

Niagara Falls, 1994   Photo: LEF 1994

NIAGARA FALLS

Nature's Wonder

~~~~~~~~~~~~~~~~

LEONARD EVERETT FISHER

Holiday House/New York

Horseshoe Falls seen from American side, 1994   *Photo: LEF 1994*

To my grandchildren, with love:

Samuel	*Benjamin*
Gregory	*Byron*
Jordan	*Lucas*
Lauren	*Nicole*
Danielle	*Olivia*

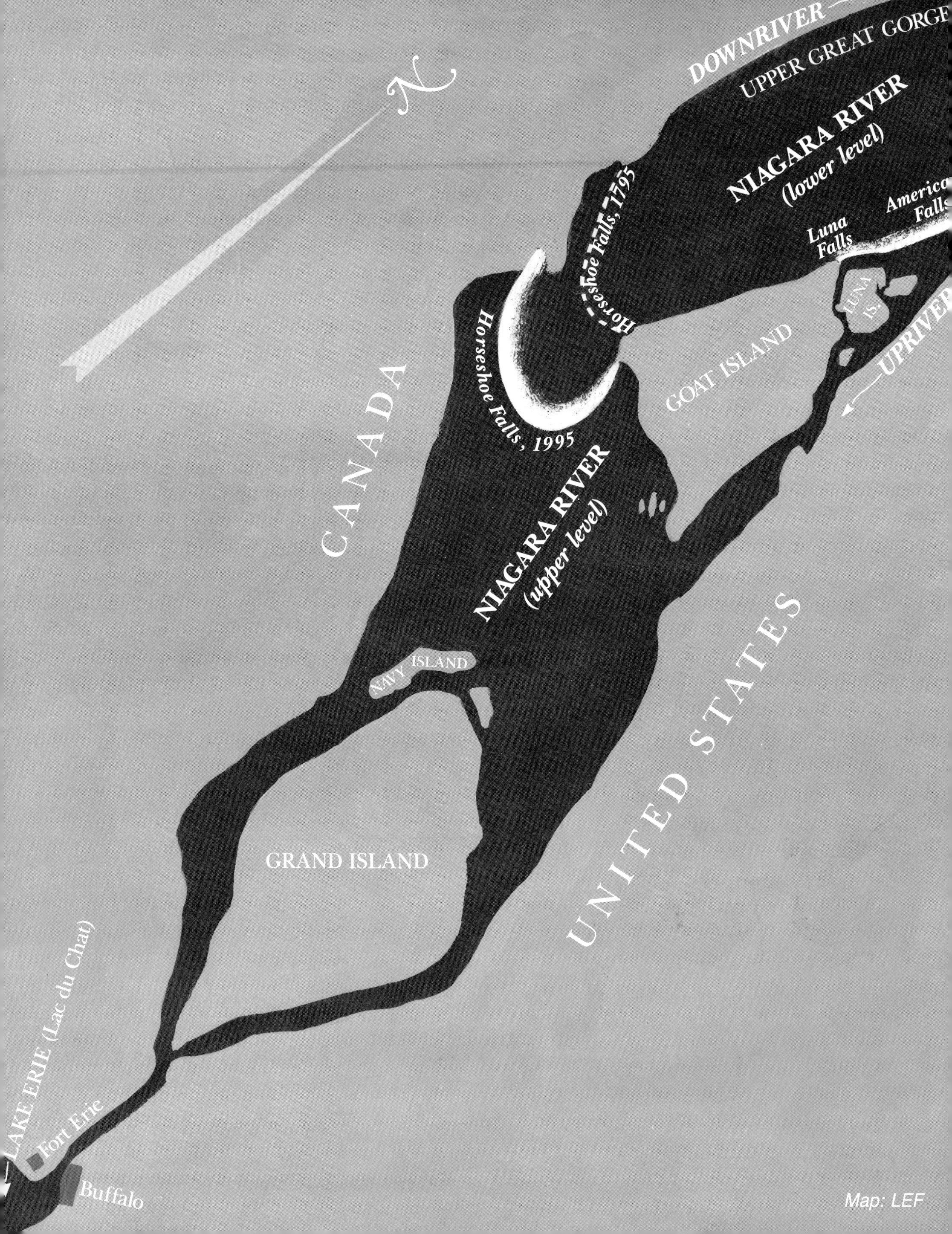

DOWNRIVER →

UPPER GREAT GORGE

NIAGARA RIVER
(lower level)

Luna Falls

America Falls

N

Horseshoe Falls, 1795

Horseshoe Falls, 1795

LUNA IS.

GOAT ISLAND

← UPRIVER

CANADA

Horseshoe Falls, 1995

NIAGARA RIVER
(upper level)

UNITED STATES

NAVY ISLAND

GRAND ISLAND

LAKE ERIE (Lac du Chat)

Fort Erie

Buffalo

Map: LEF

TO ST. CATHARINES

Rainbow Bridge

Whirlpool Bridge

WHIRLPOOL RAPIDS GORGE

Whirlpool

Devil's Hole

Robert Moses Power Plant

Eldridge Terrace

Lewiston-Queenston Bridge

Ontario Hydro Electric Power Plant

Roy Terrace

Queenston

Lewiston

Fort Niagara

Fort George

LAKE ONTARIO (Lac de Frontenac)

"Four leagues from Lac de Frontenac," wrote an awestruck French Franciscan friar named Louis Hennepin, "there is an incredible . . . Waterfall, which has no equal."

Father Hennepin did not exaggerate when he told of finding immense tumbles of water in North America that "foam and boil in a fearful manner." He was the first European to announce the existence of Niagara Falls in *Description de la Louisiane*, an account of his travels, published in France in 1683.

The thirty-eight-year-old priest and La Motte de Lussière, captain of a small sailing ship, together with its crew, had been scouting the Niagara River in December 1678, when they came upon the falls. De Lussière was one of a group of young noblemen employed by René-Robert Cavelier, Sieur de la Salle (1643–1687), a high-born but nearly impoverished French adventurer. Father Hennepin was his personal chaplain.

La Salle, who had stayed behind on the rim of Lac de Frontenac, now Lake Ontario, had sent de Lussière, accompanied by Father Hennepin, to the mouth of the river. From there they sailed south against the current of the river flowing north from Lake Erie, which the French called Lac du Chat, "Lake of the Cat." After traveling a short distance, they saw the spectacular waterfalls, whose roar they had already heard previously when they had approached the mouth of the river.

Father Hennepin would later write that "when the wind blows in a southerly direction the noise they make is heard for more than fifteen leagues."

The French had been exploring the Great Lakes and Niagara regions since 1534, when Jacques Cartier arrived in what is now Quebec, Canada, and claimed the vast area for France. But before he and other Europeans had even set foot in North

America, Native American Indians living around the eastern Great Lakes knew about the great, thunderous, crashing cascades of water that lay near and between what is presently Buffalo, New York, and St. Catharines, Canada.

In the 1500s five squabbling tribes of the Great Lakes region—the Seneca, Mohawk, Cayuga, Onondaga, and Oneida—had formed a loose confederation. Another group of tribes, the Wendat or Huron, whom they despised, called them Iruqwoy, a Wendat word for "serpent." The French spelled out the sound of the name as "Iroquois." Later British colonizers called these Iroquoian-speaking tribes "The Five Nations." One of these tribes or "nations," the Seneca, controlled the area around Niagara Falls.

In the early 1700s, English settlers succeeded in driving the Iroquoian-speaking Tuscarora Indians from their lands in the Carolinas. The Five Nations invited the Tuscarora to join their league. In 1722, the Tuscarora moved north and settled in the Niagara Falls area.

The Seneca, and later the Tuscarora, traveled along a dirt trail by the edge of the Niagara River. The trail followed the south-to-north flow of the water from Lake Erie to Lake Ontario. At a spot some twenty-three miles from Lake Erie, the land fell straight away. There, the river dove into a gaping space, smashing into the rock-strewn bottom below, then leaped northward toward Lake Ontario.

The Indians traveled back and forth, north and south, clambering up and down the banks of the falls. They clutched the steep and fast-dropping land with their hands and feet, or climbed a series of ladders they had made by propping trees against the cliffs.

If they traveled by canoe instead of by foot, they took their boat out of the water. They lugged it, along with its contents,

8

up and down the trail, through the bordering brush, to the upper or lower level of the river. There, at either level, they refloated the canoe. The process of carrying boats and supplies overland between two bodies of water is called "portage." The portage between the two levels of the river was extremely dangerous because of the steep climbs in either direction.

The south-to-north trip on the river was the least difficult, since the canoers paddled with the flow of the water. Traveling in the opposite direction was a different matter. The canoers had a tougher time paddling upstream against the powerful downward flow of the water coming from the falls. The forces of the whirlpool prevented any canoe travel at the lower level. Indians bypassed the whirlpool by carrying their boats on the portage road long before Father Hennepin arrived in a sailing vessel.

The part of the dirt trail on the east side of the river that became a portage road extended some nine miles between the southern approach to the falls and the present-day city of Queenston, downriver.

During the French and Indian War (1754–1763), known in Canada as the Seven Years' War, France and England fought for ownership of Canada. The British used the portage road to bring supplies to Fort Niagara at the northern end of the river. For the most part, the Iroquois league sided with the British. But there were some Seneca warriors who did not. This group attacked the British. In 1763, a terrible Seneca massacre occurred at Devil's Hole, about four miles north of the falls on the river's east side. The British lost approximately eighty men. As a result, British army engineers built a series of log blockhouses along the road. And they added Fort Erie at the southern end of the river.

The plunging, roaring sheets of the falls crashed from the

considerable height of one river level to another river level below.

Lake Erie, the immediate source of the Niagara River at its southern end, is 578.5 feet above sea level.

Lake Ontario, thirty-five miles away at the mouth of the river at its northern end, is 246 feet above sea level, or 332.5 feet lower.

Just beyond its Lake Erie source, six-mile-wide Grand Island divides the river into two quiet streams of water moving northward. Once past Grand Island, the river unites again into a single stream until it reaches Goat Island. There it separates into American Falls, and Canadian or Horseshoe Falls. Smaller islands, such as Luna and Navy islands, are set in the river's flow above both falls.

American Falls, which also include at their southerly edge the lesser, Luna or Bridal Veil Falls, are 180 feet high, about the height of a sixteen-story building. They are 1,100 feet wide. Horseshoe Falls are some 170 feet high, but 2,500 feet wide—almost a half mile. Together they comprise Niagara Falls, one of the mightiest natural wonders and sources of energy on earth.

There are higher waterfalls in North America that spill from soaring cliffs and mountains. But none are as wide, as powerful, as full of water, or as majestic as these.

"A man who has never looked on Niagara," wrote Thomas Babington Macaulay in 1843 after having seen the falls for the first time, "has but a faint idea of a cataract."

The simple words of Lord Macaulay, the brilliant English essayist and member of Parliament, added to the falls' reputation. His words served to stir further the public desire to visit and experience the extraordinary sight that he had described.

11

American Falls, 1994   *Photo: LEF 1994*

Horseshoe Falls seen from Canadian side
Niagara Parks Commission

In 1765, seventy-eight years before Macaulay's humble observation, America's own Benjamin Franklin wrote a letter to a London newspaper. In it Franklin complained that the English were so ignorant of America, they would believe any tall tale that came from such a primeval and mysterious continent full of wonder and savagery. Franklin told them a whopper when he noted the following in his letter:

"The grand leap of the whale up the fall of Niagara, is esteemed by all who have seen it, as one of the finest spectacles in nature."

Niagara Falls seen today is no longer in the same place that Father Hennepin, Benjamin Franklin, or Lord Macaulay reported it. Nor does it look quite the same. Until about 1795, Horseshoe Falls had been located farther downriver. American Falls hardly existed. The power of the water coursing over Niagara's brink eroded much of the rocky cliff hidden beneath its flow. The erosion caused Horseshoe Falls to gradually recede to a new position more than nine hundred feet back, creating American Falls in the process. This backward march over 200 years—which continues at the rate of between four and six feet a year—produced an increasingly wider brink than what Father Hennepin saw.

At their birth twelve thousand years ago, the falls were seven miles down the Niagara River from where they are today. The actual spot on the Canadian side is near Queenston, at a place called Roy Terrace. The site was named for Dr. Roy Spencer, a geologist who first explained the natural events that created the Niagara River and Falls. Across the river and opposite Roy Terrace is Eldridge Terrace, the eastern edge of the original falls.

The landscape keeps changing, too. Table Rock, a great, flat, stony platform near Horseshoe Falls, had once reached

View Below Table Rock: engraving by William Henry Bartlett, 1840
Buffalo and Erie County Historical Society

out over the river far below. Sightseers could stand there or sit in their carriages and marvel at the spectacle of the falls. In June 1850, a sizable piece of the rock broke away and fell into the river. Eventually more of it would crumble.

Thousands of years ago, Table Rock had been part of the river's original bottom before any waterfalls existed. When a section of the land, including the riverbed, sank to a new, lower position, the falls appeared. A hunk of that bottom, Table Rock, remained high and dry above.

The same thing happened to Prospect Point, a spot on the northern crest of American Falls. Late one July afternoon in 1954, Prospect Point—185,000 tons of rock—broke away. Much of the debris landed at the base of the falls. Some of it washed downriver. The shape of American Falls was changed forever in a continuing geologic process.

The smaller American Falls are part of the United States. The larger Canadian Falls (Horseshoe Falls) belong to Canada. Most of the Niagara River's water pours over Horseshoe Falls at about 342,000 tons a minute. A white rainbowed mist always shrouds its base.

A lesser amount of water, about 38,000 tons a minute, roars over the brink of American and Luna Falls and crashes into the 170-foot-deep Upper Great Gorge. There it meets the roaring, onrushing waters of Horseshoe Falls, which are as high as the gorge is deep. This great flow of moving water squeezes into the narrow Whirlpool Rapids Gorge, where it churns itself farther downriver before spilling into Lake Ontario.

The Niagara River, its upper level only twenty feet deep in most places, forms a border between the United States and Canada. It was created toward the end of the Pleistocene Epoch, the most recent Ice Age. The geologic process that produced the falls, which began about 25,000 years ago, took some 13,000 years.

The Pleistocene Epoch had its beginnings almost two million years ago. During that time huge glaciers, nearly two miles thick, covered much of North America and other parts of the Northern Hemisphere. In a constantly grinding movement, the glaciers gouged out great chunks of earth beneath them.

When the cold earth became warmer, the glaciers began to melt. As the melting glaciers grew smaller and moved northward toward the polar cap, they left various sizes of depressions or basins in the land, covering tens of thousands of square miles. These basins filled with water from the melting glaciers, creating thousands of large and small freshwater lakes. Among these were the Great Lakes, the world's largest bodies of fresh water that are connected to one another. Except for Lake Michigan, which lies wholly within the United States, these giant inland freshwater seas—Lakes Superior, Huron, Erie, and Ontario—share common borders between the United States and Canada.

Millions of tons of water from the upper lakes drained into Lake Erie. Overflowing water from Lake Erie, seeking its own outlet, formed the Niagara River, which flowed into Lake Ontario. The overflow from Lake Ontario created the St. Lawrence River, which carried this titanic amount of water northeastward to the Atlantic Ocean. And the process continues.

The Seneca had their own ideas, or so the story goes, about what shaped Niagara Falls (especially Horseshoe Falls). In the Iroquoian language, *niagara* means "thunder of water." The Seneca used the word to describe the thunderous roar of their sacred falls, whose waters they worshiped as the god Hinu.

The French mistakenly interpreted *niagara* as meaning "throat," which they used as an image to portray the thirty-five-mile river passage between Lakes Erie and Ontario. Perhaps some ancient Seneca storyteller passed the tale on like this:

Long before the white man came to our land and waterways, we lived in fear of Hinu, the Thunder God. Hinu lives with two sons in the caves behind the falls. Everyone hears him, since his voice is the great roar of the falls. To keep Hinu happy and well fed, we sent canoes full of food over the falling waters.

Once a terrible sickness visited our people. Many died. Someone plowed under our burial grounds and ate our dead. Everyone thought that Hinu had become angry with us, that Hinu had done this to us. Why? We had no idea. To soothe his anger, not only did we send more canoes full of food over the falls, but we also sacrificed our daughters. The young girls were caught in Hinu's embrace—swallowed up by the rushing water—never to be seen again.

One day, a chief sacrificed his daughter. She fell over the falls into the arms of one of Hinu's sons. But the chief changed his mind and wanted his daughter back. He took his canoe over the running water to find her. He was captured by Hinu, never again to be seen or heard.

Meanwhile, his daughter had already promised to marry Hinu's son if only he would tell her why so many of our people had to die and be eaten in their graves.

Hinu's son declared it was not his father, the Thunder God, who did these foul things. It was a hungry monster in the river, a great water snake that rose out of the river to poison us and eat our dead.

Hearing this, the spirit of the chief's daughter floated out of the

20

Horseshoe Falls seen from the lower Niagara River, 1994   *Photo: LEF 1994*

mist that hid the falling water and returned to our people. She told us about the terrible water snake and the hour that the monster would strike next.

When the water snake rose out of the river and struck, just as she had predicted, we wounded it. We took its still live and squirming body to the brink of the plunging water. We placed its head between two rocks on one side and its tail between two rocks on the other side. There, stretched in the shape of a great horseshoe across both sides of the waterway, the monster died. The water rushed over its stiff, curved body as it does to this very day.

The spirit of the chief's daughter returned to Hinu's son. She still lives happily in the caves behind the falling waters and has been known from that day to this as "Maid of the Mist."

There is neither an ancient Seneca oral tradition nor written record of this tale. Some say the legend was invented by enterprising American or Canadian businessmen to attract crowds of tourists to Niagara Falls, where they would spend plenty of money. Some versions call the Thunder God "Hinum" rather than "Hinu." Hinum, when pronounced backwards, sounds like the English word *money*.

The use of the term *horseshoe* in describing the Canadian Falls came from versions of the Seneca legend in which the storyteller compared the curve of the dead water snake to that of a horseshoe. Assuming that the legend is ancient enough to predate the arrival of white men to North America, neither the Seneca nor any other Native American could have known a horseshoe from a horseman. There were no horses, thus no horseshoes, on the North American continent until the arrival of Europeans during the 1500s. Whatever the truth, the story, or various versions of it, has become part of the mythology of Niagara Falls.

The "Maid of the Mist," described in the legend as the spirit of the chief's daughter, is also the name of each of the small boats that take tourists nearer the falls for a better look. These boats have provided sightseers with drenching river views since 1846.

Niagara Falls tour boats had their beginnings in 1818. At that time, William Forsyth, the owner of the Pavilion Hotel on the Canadian side, and Parkhurst Whitney, the owner of Hotel Eagle on the American side, saw the need for a ferry service between their two countries and hotels. They built the first stairways down the banks on each side of the river to enable passengers to reach the boats. Years later, elevators would replace the stairways, while an inclined railway would bring tourists right to the boat landing.

The ferry business made it possible for passengers to be rowed across the river for fares that ranged between twelve-and-a-half to twenty-five cents. There was an extra charge for baggage, and still another charge if the passengers wanted to be rowed upriver to get a closer look at the falls. As the stairways to the ferry landings were improved, roads were cut into the steep embankments to create better access to the boats.

In 1846, the first *Maid of the Mist* was put into service. She was a wooden, one-hundred-ton, coal-fed, steam-driven boat. The *Maid of the Mist* was designed to carry goods for sale across the river and to ferry the growing crush of people coming to visit the falls.

Two years later, on July 31, 1848, an 8-foot-wide, 762-foot-long suspension bridge was built across the river below the falls at their narrowest point. The bridge opened the following day, August 1. It was designed and constructed by Charles Ellett, Jr., a Philadelphia engineer. While the bridge was being built, a specially designed car hanging from a cable was

Niagara Falls ferry broadside, 1856   *New York State Library*

Maid of the Mist III, 1950   *Niagara Parks Commission*

Suspension Bridge under construction showing Ellett's Basket, 1848
Buffalo and Erie County Historical Society

strung across the river to transport workers and equipment. It also carried tourists from one side of the river to the other.

A few months before the opening of the bridge, the Upper Niagara River stopped running. On March 29, a great ice jam on Lake Erie at the mouth of the Niagara River blocked lake water from entering the river for more than twenty-four hours. In an instant, the falls became a mere trickle, nearly bone dry. Their familiar roar had been silenced. The local people and whatever sightseers were on hand to witness that shocking event could walk along what had been the brink of the falls.

"Huge fields of muddy bottom were laid bare," according to the *Buffalo Express* (March 31, 1848).

The next day, March 30, a shifting wind unjammed the ice pack. A mammoth wall of ice, water, and debris pounded down the dry upper riverbed. The Niagara River flowed once more in all its power and glory. And once more the deafening roar of the falls could be heard. All was normal again. Everyone breathed a sigh of relief.

During the 1960s, engineers developed and put in place an "ice boom," a series of long, thick timbers to control the ice flow on Lake Erie. The boom allowed the Niagara River to keep running and the Niagara cataracts to keep falling, despite icy weather conditions. Still, there were and are times in which the Niagara River is held fast in winter's freezing grip, and bridges of ice connect the Canadian side with the American side. These crushing blocks of ice are so thick that a person could easily walk across them from one riverbank to the other.

In 1912, such an ice bridge broke apart, with Sunday strollers stranded on the moving blocks. Four people on one block were swiftly carried into the Whirlpool Rapids, whose own

Ice Bridge seen from Canadian side, circa 1890–1900   *New York Public Library Picture Collection*

fury had prevented ice from forming. Only one individual was rescued. The other three drowned.

In 1848, the steamboat ferry business was all but ruined by the new and safer man-made bridge. People could now either walk across a structure spanning the river that ran between Canada and the United States, or ride "Ellett's Basket."

Sixty-eight years later, on August 8, 1916, the Spanish Aero Car began operating. Suspended on cables 250 feet above the whirlpool, the forty-passenger car gave sightseers a thrilling view of Niagara Falls, the river, and its whirlpool. The car was designed and built by Spanish engineer Leonardo Torres-Quevedo. Originally owned by a Spanish company, the car became the property of Canada's Niagara Parks Commission in 1968.

A final, crushing blow to the *Maid of the Mist* ferry business came in 1855, when John Augustus Roebling, a forty-nine-year-old American engineer who had emigrated to the United States in 1837 from Mülhausen, Germany, completed the construction of a railroad suspension bridge over the Niagara River below the falls.

Roebling's Railroad Suspension Bridge, the second bridge to span the Niagara River, remained intact for twenty-two years. During that time engines, freight, and passenger cars had become heavier and more numerous. The bridge had become less and less able to withstand the stress of the increasing traffic and load.

Between 1877 and 1886, the Roebling's Railroad Suspension Bridge was completely rebuilt, making it the third bridge over the Niagara. Ten years later, a newer, nonsuspension, steel-arch railroad bridge was built around it, without interrupting any rail traffic that was still traveling across the river on Roebling's suspension bridge.

top: Ellett's Suspension Bridge, 1848

bottom: Roebling's Railroad Suspension Bridge, 1855

Royal Ontario Museum

National Archives of Canada

Spanish Aero Car over the whirlpool, 1916   *Niagara Parks Commission*

Designed by Leiffert L. Buck, the civil engineer who had re-designed Roebling's suspension bridge, the newer arch bridge replaced both Roebling's bridge and its renovation. The new bridge became the fourth one over the Niagara River.

Over the next half century, more bridges were built below the falls to absorb the steadily increasing traffic between Canada and the United States. Among the more notable of these were the Rainbow Bridge, completed in 1941, and the identically designed Queenston-Lewiston Bridge, which opened in 1962.

The Rainbow Bridge, an arched span, replaced the forty-three-year-old, swaying, rotted Upper Steel Arch Bridge, which was finally loosened from its moorings by ice. Since its opening, the Rainbow Bridge has been a symbol of peace and cooperation between Canada and the United States.

The Queenston-Lewiston Bridge was also constructed to replace an aging Whirlpool Rapids Bridge, a suspension span about five miles to its south.

During the mid-nineteenth century, while rowboats continued to take people across the Niagara River, the *Maid of the Mist* began a new business—taking people on tours of the falls.

Not only were visitors anxious to approach the falls as near as they dared. They also wanted to get behind the falls and tour the drenching, cold wet caves hidden by the falling sheets of water.

In 1753, an adventuresome Canadian, Monsieur Bonne-fons, climbed down to the riverbank below Table Rock. Defying the drenching, thunderous spray, he inched his way to the base of Horseshoe Falls and somehow found a route that put him behind the falls. There he discovered a large cavern.

Some time after 1818, a set of wood stairs was built leading down to the bank where only the most daring would venture

Maid of the Mist boarding area on the American side, 1994 *Photo: LEF 1994*

to the cavern behind the falls. But these brave souls could not get past a rocky formation called Termination Rock, which blocked any subterranean passage beyond the cavern. During the 1830s, an official Termination Rock Certificate was presented to anyone who had "passed behind the great falling sheet of water."

So many visitors had flocked to Niagara Falls by the 1830s that a guidebook, *Steel's Guide to Niagara Falls,* was published to point out Niagara's attractions. These included not only the cavern, Termination Rock, and a museum but also a stream of ignitable gas called the Burning Spring. The gas escaped from a fissure at the river's edge not far from Horseshoe Falls. One enterprising man, M. J. Conklin, collected the rising gas in a barrel through whose top protruded a tube. For twelve-and-a-half cents, Mr. Conklin would pass a lighted candle through a jet of gas coming from the tube. The gas would burst into a bright flame to the delight of the paying customer, until Mr. Conklin shut it off each time by pinching the tube.

In 1855, another entrepreneur, Thomas Barnett, built a tunnel below Table Rock to allow sightseers to "pass behind the great Horseshoe Falls," as he advertised, "and view one of the grandest sights of nature." Barnett charged admission for guided tours through his tunnel and provided water-protection clothing for his visitors.

Not all the crossings and viewings of the Niagara River and Falls, however, were so calm and successful.

In 1837, the year that Roebling immigrated to America, a series of rebellious events in Canada, then a British colony, had shaken the British home government. The French had lost Canada to Great Britain seventy-four years before in the final battle of the French and Indian War (Seven Years' War).

Now another fight was brewing, this time a rebellion. A

36

Termination Rock Certificate, 1838   *New York Public Library Picture Collection*

NIAGARA FALLS, U. C.

This is to certify, that Thomas
S. Woodcock

has passed behind the great falling
SHEET OF WATER,
to " Termination Rock."

Given under my hand, at
the office of the General Register
of the Names of Visitors at the
Table Rock
This 30 day of May 183 6

Ha Trackly

group disloyal to the Crown and led by William Lyon Mackenzie wanted to break away from England. They wanted an independent republican form of government for Canada, similar to that of the United States.

Mackenzie's rebel troops had moved onto Navy Island in the Niagara River. They were using it as a base of operations against Canada. An American steamboat, *The Caroline*, sailing out of Buffalo, New York, was supplying them with arms. In the black of night, December 29, 1837, Canadian troops loyal to the Crown crossed the Niagara River, entered United States territory, and captured *The Caroline*. The vessel was set on fire and sank. One American was killed.

The invasion of the United States territory by British-Canadian forces was seen as an act of war. United States troops were rushed to the border. Americans, sympathetic to Mackenzie's rebellion and still wary of British intentions in North America, demanded war with England. American-British relations had not been altogether smooth since the American Revolution and the War of 1812, in which British soldiers burned the White House in Washington, D.C. The incident on the Niagara created a difficult situation. It took five years for tempers between the United States and British Canada to finally cool.

Despite occasional flare-ups on the American-Canadian border, painters, and later photographers, visited the Niagara River. The extraordinary sight of the falls fueled their imaginations.

The earliest of these artists was Father Hennepin himself, who recorded the presence of the falls with sketches. A number of early English artists, like R. Hancock, used the Hennepin sketches from which to make engravings. Some of these early artists were English army officers stationed on the Ca-

William Lyon MacKenzie   *Archives of Ontario*

nadian side of the falls. They, as well as American army officers, were taught as cadets to make watercolor sketches of terrain for military purposes.

In about 1800, George Heriot (1766–1844), the British deputy postmaster of Canada, educated in a royal military academy where he studied watercolor sketching, made numerous such paintings while surveying places for postal services. Among his sketches were those of Niagara Falls.

The first American to paint the falls was John Vanderlyn (1775–1852). Vanderlyn had spent a good deal of time in Europe refining his considerable talent. The paintings he created of Niagara Falls (1801–1802) were taken to London and became the basis for engravings. These engravings were widely circulated and received a good deal of attention, as did the original paintings. They did much to expand the public's impression of the site. Vanderlyn, probably the first "professional" American artist to paint the falls, profited little from his works. He died poor and unknown.

Writers, too, came to stare at the splendor of so much rushing, plunging water. And when they left, they expressed in words their own passion for the sound, sight, and rhythmical fury of the falls.

"I have seen the Falls and am all rapture and amazement," wrote Thomas Moore, the Irish poet, in 1804. "I felt as if approaching the very residence of the Deity; the tears started into my eyes . . . the most burning words of poetry have all been lavished upon inferior and ordinary subjects. We must have new . . . language to describe the Falls of Niagara."

Scientists came seeking explanations of nature's mysterious workings. Engineers arrived who were interested in discovering ways to control the power of the falls. Honeymooning couples' passion for each other was served by the sheer beauty

top: Waterfalls of Niagara: engraving by R. Hancock, 1794,
         after sketch by Father Louis Hennepin
                                                          National Archives of Canada

bottom: A View of the Western Branch of the Falls of the
         Niagara: an oil painting by John Vanderlyn, circa 1802
         Note Table Rock in the foreground.
                                                          National Archives of Canada

of the falls. Entrepreneurs—hotelkeepers, food vendors, guides, carriage drivers or "hackmen," bridge builders, acrobats, daredevil men and women, publicity seekers—dreamed of the fortunes to be made from tourists, local businessmen, and the curious. Finally, architects made plans for building sky-reaching towers to give everyone uncluttered views of the vastness of the remarkable Niagara Falls.

By the 1850s, the Seneca and other Native Americans, who had lived around Niagara Falls for centuries, became a dwindling people. Tribal and colonial wars, disease, and the white man had overwhelmed them.

Following the Civil War (1861–1865), Niagara Falls became the destination of thousands of sightseers from everywhere in the world.

Upon seeing Niagara Falls for the first time in 1871, one famous visitor, Samuel Clemens—otherwise known as Mark Twain—was greatly moved by the experience. But he was irritated no end by the sightseers who covered the area like so many "reptiles" and "worms," as they blocked and tarnished the numbing beauty of the falls.

In his *Sketches New and Old*, published thirty-two years later, in 1903, he wrote:

> *Any day, in the hands of these photographers, you may see stately pictures of Papa and Mama, Johnny and Bub and Sis, or a couple of country cousins, all smiling vacantly, and all disposed in studied and uncomfortable attitudes in their carriage, and all looming up in their awe-inspiring imbecility before that majestic presence whose ministering spirits are the rainbows, whose voice is the thunder, whose awful front is veiled in clouds, who was monarch here dead and forgotten ages before this hackful of small reptiles was deemed temporarily necessary to fill a crack in the*

Tourists at Niagara Falls, circa 1850   *Archives of Ontario*

world's unnoted myriads, and will still be monarch here ages and decades of ages after they shall have gathered themselves to their blood relations, the other worms, and been mingled with the un-remembering dust.

Poet Morris Bishop, who followed Samuel Clemens to Niagara, was just as critical of the Niagara Falls tourist. He later expressed his contempt in his *Public Aid for Niagara Falls:*

> There I stood, and humbly scanned
> The miracle that sense appals,
> And I watched the tourists stand
> Spitting in Niagara Falls.

Among those who called attention to Niagara Falls were the men and women who viewed the falls as the greatest theatrical stage in the world. They ignored the danger of the falls and the river with daring, death-defying stunts. And each tried to outdo the other. Many had little regard for their personal safety.

Some walked above the Whirlpool Rapids on taut ropes and high wires. Others squeezed into a barrel, looking death in the face as they let the furious whirlpool, averaging twenty-four and a half feet deep, whip their bruising bodies from one side of the river to the other. And there were those who refused to be outdone by a mere whirlpool or high-wire circus act. They slid down the river in their barrels and plunged over the falls in tooth-rattling, bone-chilling seconds.

The earliest of these daredevils was Samuel Patch, a high-jumping athlete of sorts. In 1829, Sam erected a ladder at the river's edge beneath Goat Island, about halfway between American and Horseshoe Falls. The ladder was at least a hundred feet high. The huge crowd that came to see him jump filled the inns and several hotels. Business boomed. At the appointed hour, Sam climbed to the top of his ladder and jumped into the river. Having survived that heart-stopping dive, he climbed the ladder again and jumped once more, swimming away from still another heart-stopping dive.

Thirty years later, Sam Patch's spectacular dive would be eclipsed by a French actor, Jean François Gravelet, who called himself "Blondin." On June 30, 1859, Blondin, dressed in tights, walked a tightrope almost 200 feet above the gorge. Ten thousand spectators cheered him on. He even drank a bottle of wine in the twenty minutes that it took for him to carefully work his way across the 1,100-foot span from the American to the Canadian side. The return trip took eight minutes.

Blondin continued to walk the rope all summer long, earning his fortune from the hotel owners and the collections taken up by the crowd that passed the hat on his behalf. On one occasion, 50,000 people held their collective breath as they watched him cross the river on the tightrope, carrying his manager on his back. And just to prove that he could do such a thing anytime he chose, he carried his assistant on his back on another day.

During the summer of 1860, Blondin was challenged by a Canadian "ropewalker," William Hunt. Using the name "Signor Farini," Hunt did everything he could to draw the great crowds away from Blondin. Performing on a nearby rope, Farini made sure to outdo Blondin on the very day and at the very same time that Blondin performed. When Blondin announced he would take a stove with him on the rope and cook a meal, Farini carried a washtub on the rope and washed some handkerchiefs, hanging them out to dry on his balancing pole.

45

next page: Blondin Crossing Niagara Falls on a Tightrope: detail from an oil painting thought to be by Seth Eastman, circa 1859-1860

Collection of the New York Historical Society

Farini Broadside, 1860   *Buffalo and Erie County Historical Society*

Blondin and Farini become so famous, they attracted a visit from England's Prince of Wales.

The competition continued all during the summer and early fall of 1860. The two acrobats would never return. Nor would the great crowds, at least not for a few more years. In 1861, Confederate forces in South Carolina fired on the Union's Fort Sumter. The Civil War had begun. Few tourists came to Niagara Falls during the next four years of the bitter American conflict. After the war, a number of other ropewalkers and wire walkers performed their specialties across the gorge. Several achieved almost as much fame as Blondin and Farini.

In 1876, twenty-three-year-old Maria Spelterini, a circus performer, was the first woman to cross the gorge on a tightrope. Blindfolded, it took her eleven minutes to walk before an audience of thousands of people. On the return trip, she removed the blindfold and did the walk backwards in fifteen minutes. During another one of her excursions, she wore a wood peach basket on each foot.

Clifford Calverley, a tightwire walker, was even more daring. In 1892, he carried a chair as he gingerly crossed the gorge on his wire. About halfway across, Calverley placed the chair on the wire and sat on it. He took his ease while reading a newspaper and smoking a cigarette.

The last of the rope and wire performers was Oscar Williams. In 1911, Williams, billed as the "Great Houdin" (not the world-famous magician and stuntman, Harry Houdini) was prepared to cross the gorge hanging by his teeth from a leather strap attached to a wheel that ran along a stretched wire. He was supposed to slide down the wire with such speed that the momentum of the slide from the American side would be enough to have him ascend to the Canadian side.

Everything went fine as the dangling Williams whipped

Maria Spelterini crosses the Gorge, 1876   *New York Public Library Picture Collection*

down the wire. He passed the halfway point and began to ascend. But his momentum was not enough to carry him the whole way up. Instead, he rolled back to the halfway point of the wire's slack. There he stopped, dangling by his teeth above the gorge. Waiting below was the *Maid of the Mist*. After about a half hour, Williams grabbed a rope that rescuers were able to get to him and safely descended to the deck of the boat.

In 1875, Matthew Webb, a celebrated deepwater swimmer, successfully swam the dangerous English Channel. In July 1883, Webb tried to swim the Whirlpool Rapids and quickly drowned. Three years later, Carlisle Graham was able to cross the river through the whirlpool in a barrel. In fact he did it four times and was hailed as the "Hero of the Niagara."

Between 1886 and 1901, a number of people crossed the whirlpool in barrels. Among this group were three women, Maude Willard, Martha Wagenfuhrer, and Sadie Allen.

Maude Willard sealed herself in a barrel with her dog. The dog survived, but Maude did not. She died of suffocation. Her dog had stuck his nose in the barrel's airhole, cutting off her only air supply. Martha Wagenfuhrer crossed the whirlpool alone in the same barrel and lived. Sadie Allen survived the trip when she went through the whirlpool with a friend, William Hazlett.

By the turn of the century, crossing the Whirlpool Rapids in a barrel had lost its appeal for those who sought greater Niagara adventure and the fame and money that came with more danger. Other than the unfortunate and unnecessary death of Maude Willard, the challenge of the whirlpool posed a lesser risk than the falls themselves. People continued to ride the whirlpool in boats, barrels, and rafts for most of the twentieth century.

In August 1972, a company was formed to take tourists

through the Whirlpool Rapids in rubber rafts. The operation lasted a month. Too many tourists were flung from the rafts into the swirling, choppy, ice-cold water. Luckily, some were able to swim to safety. Others, clinging to debris, were swept downriver into the waiting boats and arms of rescuers. Fortunately, no lives were lost.

Three years later, another company tried the same thing with what they considered better-designed rafts. They did not last long either. They were able to negotiate the rapids with ten hair-raising rides. On the eleventh ride, thirty-two people were thrown from one raft. This time three people died. The company, Niagara Gorge River Trips, shut down its business.

Carlisle Graham, the early Hero of the Niagara, began looking at the falls as the ultimate challenge. What would happen if he took himself over Horseshoe Falls in a barrel? No one had ever done that before! He wasted so much time talking about his plan instead of carrying it out, however, that Annie Taylor, a schoolteacher from Bay City, Michigan, beat him to it. Lusting for fame and fortune beyond the classroom, she wasted no time in deciding how to achieve both.

Late in the afternoon of October 24, 1901, Annie Taylor's manager set her adrift above Horseshoe Falls in a five-and-a-half-foot-long padded barrel. Eighteen minutes later, Annie Taylor went over the falls. The barrel was weighted with a heavy iron anvil at its bottom so that Annie would not only be upright during the less-than-fifteen-second descent, but remain upright as she floated on the river below. A special harness kept her from rattling around inside the barrel. Although air had been pumped into the barrel after it was sealed, Annie breathed through a rubber hose she held in her mouth. The hose was connected to a hole in the barrel.

Annie Taylor survived the breathtaking descent, the first

The Great Gorge Rapids
Niagara Parks Commission

and only woman to do it alone. Carlisle Graham never made the attempt. Now he was no longer the Hero of the Niagara. But while Annie found fame as "Queen of the Mist," she died penniless twenty years later in a New York poorhouse.

Annie Taylor's incredible accomplishment inspired others to repeat the feat, some with better luck than others.

Bobby Leach, a fifty-two-year-old, English-born Canadian stuntman, went over Horseshoe Falls in a steel barrel on July 25, 1911. Leach had previously succeeded in making a couple of trips through the Whirlpool Rapids. He had parachuted also from the Upper Steel Arch Bridge. Bobby Leach barely survived his quick trip over the falls. Badly injured, he spent nearly six months recovering from his broken bones. For the next fifteen years, Bobby Leach went on tour all over the world with a film of his near-fatal adventure. In 1926, while on tour, he slipped on a New Zealand street and died of his injuries.

Charles G. Stephens, an English barber, went over the falls on July 11, 1925. Stephens was never found again. All that was left of him was a tattooed arm.

A great clamor developed to have both Canadian and American authorities make these plunges illegal. Eventually they did, but not for a number of years. And when a law finally did get passed that it was a misdemeanor or criminal mischief to go over the falls in any kind of contraption, the authorities did little to enforce the new statute.

Three years later, July 4, 1928, a New York machinist, Jean A. Lussier, went over Horseshoe Falls in a hard rubber ball reinforced by steel ribs. The falls pounded him downward in seconds. Two hundred thousand people cheered as Lussier climbed out of his ball, alive.

William Hill, Jr., a friend of Lussier's, challenged the falls in

Annie Taylor, "Queen of the Mist"   *Niagara Parks Commission*

1951 and died. His vehicle was a claptrap contrivance made of automobile-tire inner tubes. It was such an odd vehicle that it was called "The Thing." The local police did nothing to stop him from making the plunge, despite the fact that such stunts were now illegal.

In 1961, William Fitzgerald, also called "Nathan Boya," fell over the falls in a ball. This was not an ordinary ball. It was a scientifically engineered, plastic-coated, rubber-and-steel sphere that included snorkels, an escape hatch, an emergency air supply, carbon dioxide cans, inner-tube shock absorbers, and a well-designed harness. Fitzgerald, an employee of International Business Machines, was arrested by Canadian police and fined $113. He was the first person to have gone over the falls to have been apprehended by the police.

Between 1984 and 1995, five others climbed into their various barrel-like contraptions and traveled over Horseshoe Falls. They all made it, only to be arrested. One of these, Karel Soucek, a stuntman, was fined $500 for his 1984 trip. A year later, he climbed into a wood whiskey barrel at the top of the Astrodome in Houston, Texas. He was supposed to drop 180 feet into a water tank. He missed the tank and died.

Another daredevil, Steven Trotter, took the ride over the falls in a fifteen-foot, radio-equipped cylinder in 1985. He had to pay two fines: $500 to the Canadians for doing what was now prohibited, and $5,000 to the Americans for failing to obtain a license from the Buffalo, New York, portmaster to bring a watergoing vessel into a "safety zone."

In October 1985, John David Munday, an Ontario garage owner and mechanic, went over Horseshoe Falls in a well-engineered, 725-pound plastic barrel. The barrel itself weighed only about 400 pounds. The rest of the weight was in the sand at its bottom, used to keep the tank upright, in much the same way as Annie Taylor's anchor did eighty-four years earlier. It was Munday's second attempt. He had been arrested and placed on probation for his unsuccessful first attempt. He was arrested twice after his successful second attempt—once for violating his probation and again for having gone over the falls. And he was fined as well. But John David Munday would not be the last.

Ten years later, on the morning of June 18, 1995, two young people did it in a metal cylinder and lived. It took them fifteen seconds to hit the rocky bottom of Horseshoe Falls, where they got stuck behind a boulder. It took an hour for the Niagara Park Police emergency crew to get them out. Bruised but thrilled by their success, they were arrested on the spot and carried off to a hospital on stretchers in full view of worldwide television cameras.

Besides the daredevils who looked upon the falls as a challenge, the painters and writers whose imaginations were stimulated, and the honeymooners and other tourists who were spellbound by its beauty, there were those who wanted to harness its energy.

Two American business partners, August Porter and his younger brother, United States Congressman Peter Porter, purchased land from New York State in 1805. The land extended north from the village of Buffalo on Lake Erie, running along the east side of the Niagara River above and below American Falls.

In that same year, 1805, they built a water-powered grist mill and tannery on the eastern bank of the Upper Niagara River. It was on the site of an earlier sawmill constructed by French frontiersmen. The mill operated for twenty years. There had been other earlier mills along the Upper Niagara, such as the Bridgewater Mills, that were built during the eigh-

Ontario Hydro Electric Power Plant
Ontario Hydro, Corporate Archives

teenth century. But none were operated by such visionaries as the Porter brothers. They were driven by the idea of using the entire river and its falls to provide industrial power for the immediate Niagara area and for the larger territories beyond it.

The brothers hoped that American manufacturing plants would move to Porter properties along the river, using the water as a source of mechanical power. The response was slow. The Porter brothers died. Their descendants gave up their rights to the land to various companies, such as the Niagara Falls Canal Company. These companies were run by New York and New England businessmen who focused their attention on producing cheap waterpower. But they underestimated the millions of dollars it would take to harness the power of the Niagara, and kept running out of money. They could not complete the necessary canals and reservoirs to control the massive power of the river and divert it for industrial use. Also, the Civil War disrupted some of the work, forcing these companies into bankruptcy.

The Porters' dream, however, began to take hold near the end of the century. In 1877, Joseph Schoellkopf, a Buffalo businessman, took over these failed waterpower companies. He reorganized them as the Niagara Falls Hydraulic and Manufacturing Company. He financed the company with the sale of stock to the public. Within five years, the company was operating an electric generator that was supplying waterpower to a number of area mills. The gears of turbine engines operated by waterpower made the rest of the machinery work.

The Niagara Falls Hydraulic and Manufacturing Company's generator also supplied the power for the electric generator of the Brush Electric Light and Power Company's system of arc lighting, the first of its kind in the world.

After the success of the Schoellkopf generator, Niagara projects to distribute vast amounts of power through electricity blossomed. The Niagara River Hydraulic Tunnel, Power and Sewer Company was formed, eventually becoming the Niagara Falls Power Company. It built a two-and-a-half-mile tunnel under the falls on the New York side. The tunnel housed nearly forty turbines whose combined power ran the hundreds of factories. The project was finished in 1896 when, with the flip of a switch, the entire city of Buffalo was electrified, including the running of its streetcars.

The Canadian Niagara Power Company was formed in 1888. In 1905, the Ontario Power Company began operating a generator at the foot of Horseshoe Falls. Like the Niagara Falls Power Company, tunnels bored out of hard rock and housing turbines used the immense power of the river to generate electricity on the Canadian side. Other companies were formed, including Ontario Hydro and the Electric Development Company (later called Toronto Power). They created and distributed electrical power far beyond Niagara Falls.

The delivery of electric power of such magnitude stood as an engineering marvel. It demonstrated the promise of a greater industrialization of the world itself. And this in turn held out the promise of a more comfortable life for people everywhere.

Nevertheless, while the mighty Niagara Falls allowed itself to be harnessed, it cannot be measured merely by what it can give to humankind. Its wide presence and sheer beauty are a reminder that its majesty transcends its usefulness.

All those who have experienced the falls and river, from the native Seneca and Father Hennepin to the modern tourist, bear witness to their awesomeness. And all will agree that Niagara Falls, the natural wonder, is unforgettable.

Index

(Italicized numbers indicate pages with photos.)

Library of Congress Cataloging-in-Publication Data
Fisher, Leonard Everett.
Niagara Falls : nature's wonder / Leonard Everett Fisher. — 1st ed.
p.   cm.
Includes index.
Summary: Introduces the history and lore of Niagara Falls.
ISBN 0-8234-1240-7 (hardcover : alk. paper)
1. Niagara Falls (N.Y. and Ont.)—Juvenile literature.
[1. Niagara Falls (N.Y. and Ont.)]   I. Title.
F127.N8F57   1996   95–42740   CIP   AC
971.3'39—dc20